MY AQUARIUM LOG BOOK

FISH TANK MAINTENANCE RECORD - MONITORING, FEEDING, WATER TESTING, FILTER CHANGES, AND OVERALL OBSERVATIONS

NICE AND SIMPLE PRINTS

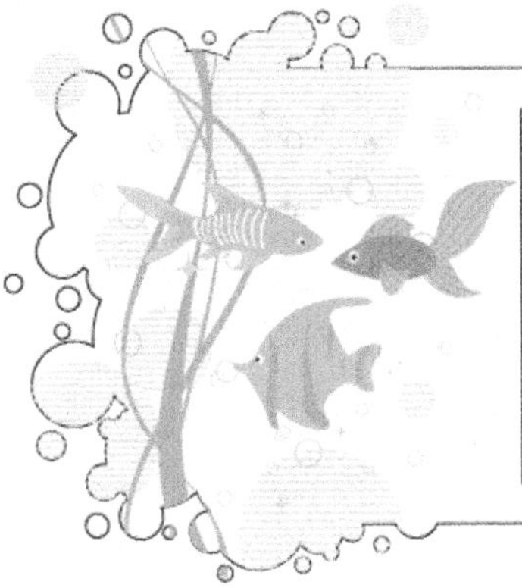

This book belonge to:

Contact Information

Address: ____________________

____

Phone: ____________________

Weekly Maintenance Log

Maintenance Parameters

Date:

Temperature:	% Water Change:
pH Levels:	Ammonia Levels:
Nitrite Levels:	Nitrate Levels:
Alkalinity Levels:	Salinity Levels:
Phosphate Levels:	Added Water Conditions: Y or N
Light Schedule Time	**Feeding Schedule Times**
ON ---------------- AM	☐ ---------------- AM
OFF ---------------- AM	☐ ---------------- PM
Other:	Other:

General Observation Notes:

Weekly Aquarium Maintenance Log

Name: ______________________________ Start Date: ____________________

Aquarium Purchasa Date: ________________ Number of Fish: ____________

Type of Fish: ____

Item	Details	MON	TUE	WED	THU	FRI	SAT	SUN
Water Change								
Vacuum Gravel								
Clean Filter								
Change Filter								
Clean Impeller								
Change Impeller								
Clean Heater								
Change Heater								
Air Stone Change								
Clean Decorations								
Temperature Check								
Feed Fish								
Fish Medication								

Days

Notes:

____

____

____

____

____

____

____

Weekly Maintenance Log

Maintenance Parameters

Date:

Temperature:	% Water Change:
pH Levels:	Ammonia Levels:
Nitrite Levels:	Nitrate Levels:
Alkalinity Levels:	Salinity Levels:
Phosphate Levels:	Added Water Conditions: Y or N
Light Schedule Time	**Feeding Schedule Times**
ON ---------------- AM	☐ ---------------- AM
OFF ----------------- AM	☐ ---------------- PM
Other:	Other:

General Observation Notes:

Weekly Aquarium Maintenance Log

Name: ______________________ Start Date: ______________________

Aquarium Purchasa Date: ______________ Number of Fish: ______________

Type of Fish: ____

Item	Details	MON	TUE	WED	THU	FRI	SAT	SUN
Water Change								
Vacuum Gravel								
Clean Filter								
Change Filter								
Clean Impeller								
Change Impeller								
Clean Heater								
Change Heater								
Air Stone Change								
Clean Decorations								
Temperature Check								
Feed Fish								
Fish Medication								

Notes:

Weekly Maintenance Log

Maintenance Parameters

Date:

Temperature:	% Water Change:
pH Levels:	Ammonia Levels:
Nitrite Levels:	Nitrate Levels:
Alkalinity Levels:	Salinity Levels:
Phosphate Levels:	Added Water Conditions: Y or N
Light Schedule Time	**Feeding Schedule Times**
ON ---------------- AM	☐ ---------------- AM
OFF ---------------- AM	☐ ---------------- PM
Other:	Other:

General Observation Notes:

Weekly Aquarium Maintenance Log

Name: ____________________ Start Date: ____________________

Aquarium Purchasa Date: ____________________ Number of Fish: ____________________

Type of Fish: ____

Item	Details	Days MON	TUE	WED	THU	FRI	SAT	SUN
Water Change								
Vacuum Gravel								
Clean Filter								
Change Filter								
Clean Impeller								
Change Impeller								
Clean Heater								
Change Heater								
Air Stone Change								
Clean Decorations								
Temperature Check								
Feed Fish								
Fish Medication								

Notes:

____

____

____

____

____

____

____

Weekly Maintenance Log

Maintenance Parameters

Date:

Temperature:	% Water Change:
pH Levels:	Ammonia Levels:
Nitrite Levels:	Nitrate Levels:
Alkalinity Levels:	Salinity Levels:
Phosphate Levels:	Added Water Conditions: [Y] or [N]
Light Schedule Time	**Feeding Schedule Times**
ON --------------- AM	[ ] --------------- AM
OFF ---------------- AM	[ ] --------------- PM
Other:	Other:

General Observation Notes:

Weekly Aquarium Maintenance Log

Name: ______________________ Start Date: ______________

Aquarium Purchasa Date: __________ Number of Fish: __________

Type of Fish: ______________________________________

Item	Details	MON	TUE	WED	THU	FRI	SAT	SUN
Water Change								
Vacuum Gravel								
Clean Filter								
Change Filter								
Clean Impeller								
Change Impeller								
Clean Heater								
Change Heater								
Air Stone Change								
Clean Decorations								
Temperature Check								
Feed Fish								
Fish Medication								

Notes:

____

____

____

____

____

____

____

Weekly Maintenance Log

Maintenance Parameters

Date:

Temperature:	% Water Change:
pH Levels:	Ammonia Levels:
Nitrite Levels:	Nitrate Levels:
Alkalinity Levels:	Salinity Levels:
Phosphate Levels:	Added Water Conditions: Y or N
Light Schedule Time	**Feeding Schedule Times**
ON ---------------- AM	☐ ---------------- AM
OFF ---------------- AM	☐ ---------------- PM
Other:	Other:

General Observation Notes:

Weekly Aquarium Maintenance Log

Name: ______________________ Start Date: ______________

Aquarium Purchasa Date: __________ Number of Fish: __________

Type of Fish: ______________________________________

Item	Details	Days MON	TUE	WED	THU	FRI	SAT	SUN
Water Change								
Vacuum Gravel								
Clean Filter								
Change Filter								
Clean Impeller								
Change Impeller								
Clean Heater								
Change Heater								
Air Stone Change								
Clean Decorations								
Temperature Check								
Feed Fish								
Fish Medication								

Notes:

Weekly Maintenance Log

Maintenance Parameters

Date:

Temperature:	% Water Change:
pH Levels:	Ammonia Levels:
Nitrite Levels:	Nitrate Levels:
Alkalinity Levels:	Salinity Levels:
Phosphate Levels:	Added Water Conditions: [Y] or [N]
Light Schedule Time	**Feeding Schedule Times**
ON ---------------- AM	[ ] ---------------- AM
OFF ---------------- AM	[ ] ---------------- PM
Other:	Other:

General Observation Notes:

Weekly Aquarium Maintenance Log

Name: ____________________ Start Date: ____________________

Aquarium Purchasa Date: ____________________ Number of Fish: ____________________

Type of Fish: ____

Item	Details	MON	TUE	WED	THU	FRI	SAT	SUN
Water Change								
Vacuum Gravel								
Clean Filter								
Change Filter								
Clean Impeller								
Change Impeller								
Clean Heater								
Change Heater								
Air Stone Change								
Clean Decorations								
Temperature Check								
Feed Fish								
Fish Medication								

Notes:

Weekly Maintenance Log

Maintenance Parameters

Date:

Temperature:

pH Levels:

Nitrite Levels:

Alkalinity Levels:

Phosphate Levels:

Light Schedule Time

ON ---------------- AM

OFF ---------------- AM

Other:

% Water Change:

Ammonia Levels:

Nitrate Levels:

Salinity Levels:

Added Water Conditions: Y or N

Feeding Schedule Times

☐ ---------------- AM

☐ ---------------- PM

Other:

General Observation Notes:

Weekly Aquarium Maintenance Log

Name: ______________________ Start Date: ______________

Aquarium Purchasa Date: ____________ Number of Fish: ____________

Type of Fish: ______________________________________

Item	Details	MON	TUE	WED	THU	FRI	SAT	SUN
Water Change								
Vacuum Gravel								
Clean Filter								
Change Filter								
Clean Impeller								
Change Impeller								
Clean Heater								
Change Heater								
Air Stone Change								
Clean Decorations								
Temperature Check								
Feed Fish								
Fish Medication								

Days

Notes:

Weekly Maintenance Log

Maintenance Parameters

Date:

Temperature:	% Water Change:
pH Levels:	Ammonia Levels:
Nitrite Levels:	Nitrate Levels:
Alkalinity Levels:	Salinity Levels:
Phosphate Levels:	Added Water Conditions: Y or N
Light Schedule Time	**Feeding Schedule Times**
ON ---------------- AM	☐ ---------------- AM
OFF ---------------- AM	☐ ---------------- PM
Other:	Other:

General Observation Notes:

Weekly Aquarium Maintenance Log

Name: ______________________ Start Date: ______________

Aquarium Purchasa Date: __________ Number of Fish: __________

Type of Fish: ______________________________________

Item	Details	MON	TUE	WED	THU	FRI	SAT	SUN
Water Change								
Vacuum Gravel								
Clean Filter								
Change Filter								
Clean Impeller								
Change Impeller								
Clean Heater								
Change Heater								
Air Stone Change								
Clean Decorations								
Temperature Check								
Feed Fish								
Fish Medication								

Notes:

____

____

____

____

____

____

____

Weekly Maintenance Log

Maintenance Parameters

Date:

Temperature:	% Water Change:
pH Levels:	Ammonia Levels:
Nitrite Levels:	Nitrate Levels:
Alkalinity Levels:	Salinity Levels:
Phosphate Levels:	Added Water Conditions: [Y] or [N]
Light Schedule Time	**Feeding Schedule Times**
ON --------------- AM	[ ] --------------- AM
OFF ---------------- AM	[ ] --------------- PM
Other:	Other:

General Observation Notes:

Weekly Aquarium Maintenance Log

Name: ______________________ Start Date: ______________

Aquarium Purchasa Date: __________ Number of Fish: __________

Type of Fish: ______________________________________

Item	Details	MON	TUE	WED	THU	FRI	SAT	SUN
Water Change								
Vacuum Gravel								
Clean Filter								
Change Filter								
Clean Impeller								
Change Impeller								
Clean Heater								
Change Heater								
Air Stone Change								
Clean Decorations								
Temperature Check								
Feed Fish								
Fish Medication								

Days

Notes:

Weekly Maintenance Log

Maintenance Parameters

Date:

Temperature:	% Water Change:
pH Levels:	Ammonia Levels:
Nitrite Levels:	Nitrate Levels:
Alkalinity Levels:	Salinity Levels:
Phosphate Levels:	Added Water Conditions: [Y] or [N]
Light Schedule Time	**Feeding Schedule Times**
ON ---------------- AM	[ ] ---------------- AM
OFF ---------------- AM	[ ] ---------------- PM
Other:	Other:

General Observation Notes:

____
____
____
____
____
____
____
____
____
____
____
____
____
____

Weekly Aquarium Maintenance Log

Name: ______________________ Start Date: ______________

Aquarium Purchasa Date: __________ Number of Fish: __________

Type of Fish: ______________________________________

Item	Details	MON	TUE	WED	THU	FRI	SAT	SUN
Water Change								
Vacuum Gravel								
Clean Filter								
Change Filter								
Clean Impeller								
Change Impeller								
Clean Heater								
Change Heater								
Air Stone Change								
Clean Decorations								
Temperature Check								
Feed Fish								
Fish Medication								

Notes:

Weekly Maintenance Log

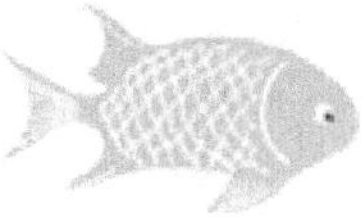

Maintenance Parameters

Date:

Temperature:	% Water Change:
pH Levels:	Ammonia Levels:
Nitrite Levels:	Nitrate Levels:
Alkalinity Levels:	Salinity Levels:
Phosphate Levels:	Added Water Conditions: Y or N
Light Schedule Time	**Feeding Schedule Times**
ON ---------------- AM	☐ ---------------- AM
OFF ---------------- AM	☐ ---------------- PM
Other:	Other:

General Observation Notes:

Weekly Aquarium Maintenance Log

Name: ______________________________ Start Date: ____________________

Aquarium Purchasa Date: ______________ Number of Fish: ______________

Type of Fish: ____

Item	Details	MON	TUE	WED	THU	FRI	SAT	SUN
Water Change								
Vacuum Gravel								
Clean Filter								
Change Filter								
Clean Impeller								
Change Impeller								
Clean Heater								
Change Heater								
Air Stone Change								
Clean Decorations								
Temperature Check								
Feed Fish								
Fish Medication								

Notes:

Weekly Maintenance Log

Maintenance Parameters

Date:

Temperature:	% Water Change:
pH Levels:	Ammonia Levels:
Nitrite Levels:	Nitrate Levels:
Alkalinity Levels:	Salinity Levels:
Phosphate Levels:	Added Water Conditions: Y or N
Light Schedule Time	**Feeding Schedule Times**
ON ---------------- AM	☐ ---------------- AM
OFF ---------------- AM	☐ ---------------- PM
Other:	Other:

General Observation Notes:

Weekly Aquarium Maintenance Log

Name: ______________________ Start Date: ______________

Aquarium Purchasa Date: __________ Number of Fish: __________

Type of Fish: ____

Item	Details	MON	TUE	WED	THU	FRI	SAT	SUN
Water Change								
Vacuum Gravel								
Clean Filter								
Change Filter								
Clean Impeller								
Change Impeller								
Clean Heater								
Change Heater								
Air Stone Change								
Clean Decorations								
Temperature Check								
Feed Fish								
Fish Medication								

Notes:

Weekly Maintenance Log

Maintenance Parameters

Date:

Temperature:	% Water Change:
pH Levels:	Ammonia Levels:
Nitrite Levels:	Nitrate Levels:
Alkalinity Levels:	Salinity Levels:
Phosphate Levels:	Added Water Conditions: Y or N
Light Schedule Time	**Feeding Schedule Times**
ON ---------------- AM	☐ ---------------- AM
OFF ---------------- AM	☐ ---------------- PM
Other:	Other:

General Observation Notes:

Weekly Aquarium Maintenance Log

Name: ______________________ Start Date: ______________

Aquarium Purchasa Date: ____________ Number of Fish: ____________

Type of Fish: ____

Item	Details	MON	TUE	WED	THU	FRI	SAT	SUN
		Days						
Water Change								
Vacuum Gravel								
Clean Filter								
Change Filter								
Clean Impeller								
Change Impeller								
Clean Heater								
Change Heater								
Air Stone Change								
Clean Decorations								
Temperature Check								
Feed Fish								
Fish Medication								

Notes:

____

____

____

____

____

____

____

Weekly Maintenance Log

Maintenance Parameters

Date:

Temperature:	% Water Change:
pH Levels:	Ammonia Levels:
Nitrite Levels:	Nitrate Levels:
Alkalinity Levels:	Salinity Levels:
Phosphate Levels:	Added Water Conditions: [Y] or [N]
Light Schedule Time	**Feeding Schedule Times**
ON --------------- AM	[ ] ---------------- AM
OFF ---------------- AM	[ ] ---------------- PM
Other:	Other:

General Observation Notes:

____

____

____

____

____

____

____

____

____

____

____

____

____

____

Weekly Aquarium Maintenance Log

Name: ______________________ Start Date: ______________

Aquarium Purchasa Date: __________ Number of Fish: __________

Type of Fish: ______________________________________

Item	Details	MON	TUE	WED	THU	FRI	SAT	SUN
Water Change								
Vacuum Gravel								
Clean Filter								
Change Filter								
Clean Impeller								
Change Impeller								
Clean Heater								
Change Heater								
Air Stone Change								
Clean Decorations								
Temperature Check								
Feed Fish								
Fish Medication								

Notes:

Weekly Maintenance Log

Maintenance Parameters

Date:

Temperature:	% Water Change:
pH Levels:	Ammonia Levels:
Nitrite Levels:	Nitrate Levels:
Alkalinity Levels:	Salinity Levels:
Phosphate Levels:	Added Water Conditions: Y or N
Light Schedule Time	**Feeding Schedule Times**
ON --------------- AM	☐ --------------- AM
OFF --------------- AM	☐ --------------- PM
Other:	Other:

General Observation Notes:

____

____

____

____

____

____

____

____

____

____

____

____

____

____

Weekly Aquarium Maintenance Log

Name: ______________________ Start Date: ______________________

Aquarium Purchasa Date: ______________ Number of Fish: ______________

Type of Fish: ____

Item	Details	MON	TUE	WED	THU	FRI	SAT	SUN
Water Change								
Vacuum Gravel								
Clean Filter								
Change Filter								
Clean Impeller								
Change Impeller								
Clean Heater								
Change Heater								
Air Stone Change								
Clean Decorations								
Temperature Check								
Feed Fish								
Fish Medication								

Days

Notes:

____

____

____

____

____

____

____

Weekly Maintenance Log

Maintenance Parameters

Date:

Temperature:	% Water Change:
pH Levels:	Ammonia Levels:
Nitrite Levels:	Nitrate Levels:
Alkalinity Levels:	Salinity Levels:
Phosphate Levels:	Added Water Conditions: Y or N
Light Schedule Time	**Feeding Schedule Times**
ON ---------------- AM	---------------- AM
OFF ----------------- AM	---------------- PM
Other:	Other:

General Observation Notes:

Weekly Aquarium Maintenance Log

Name: ______________________________ Start Date: ____________________

Aquarium Purchasa Date: ______________ Number of Fish: ______________

Type of Fish: ____

Item	Details	MON	TUE	WED	THU	FRI	SAT	SUN
Water Change								
Vacuum Gravel								
Clean Filter								
Change Filter								
Clean Impeller								
Change Impeller								
Clean Heater								
Change Heater								
Air Stone Change								
Clean Decorations								
Temperature Check								
Feed Fish								
Fish Medication								

Days

Notes:

____

____

____

____

____

____

____

Weekly Maintenance Log

Maintenance Parameters

Date:

Temperature:	% Water Change:
pH Levels:	Ammonia Levels:
Nitrite Levels:	Nitrate Levels:
Alkalinity Levels:	Salinity Levels:
Phosphate Levels:	Added Water Conditions: [Y] or [N]
Light Schedule Time	**Feeding Schedule Times**
ON ---------------- AM	[ ] ---------------- AM
OFF ----------------- AM	[ ] ---------------- PM
Other:	Other:

General Observation Notes:

Weekly Aquarium Maintenance Log

Name: ______________________ Start Date: ______________

Aquarium Purchasa Date: __________ Number of Fish: __________

Type of Fish: ____

Item	Details	MON	TUE	WED	THU	FRI	SAT	SUN
Water Change								
Vacuum Gravel								
Clean Filter								
Change Filter								
Clean Impeller								
Change Impeller								
Clean Heater								
Change Heater								
Air Stone Change								
Clean Decorations								
Temperature Check								
Feed Fish								
Fish Medication								

Notes:

Weekly Maintenance Log

Maintenance Parameters

Date:

Temperature:	% Water Change:
pH Levels:	Ammonia Levels:
Nitrite Levels:	Nitrate Levels:
Alkalinity Levels:	Salinity Levels:
Phosphate Levels:	Added Water Conditions: Y or N
Light Schedule Time	**Feeding Schedule Times**
ON ---------------- AM	☐ ---------------- AM
OFF ---------------- AM	☐ ---------------- PM
Other:	Other:

General Observation Notes:

____

____

____

____

____

____

____

____

____

____

____

____

____

____

Weekly Aquarium Maintenance Log

Name: ______________________________ Start Date: ____________________

Aquarium Purchasa Date: ______________ Number of Fish: ______________

Type of Fish: ____

Item	Details	MON	TUE	WED	THU	FRI	SAT	SUN
Water Change								
Vacuum Gravel								
Clean Filter								
Change Filter								
Clean Impeller								
Change Impeller								
Clean Heater								
Change Heater								
Air Stone Change								
Clean Decorations								
Temperature Check								
Feed Fish								
Fish Medication								

Notes:

____

____

____

____

____

____

____

Weekly Maintenance Log

Maintenance Parameters

Date:

Temperature:	% Water Change:
pH Levels:	Ammonia Levels:
Nitrite Levels:	Nitrate Levels:
Alkalinity Levels:	Salinity Levels:
Phosphate Levels:	Added Water Conditions: Y or N
Light Schedule Time	**Feeding Schedule Times**
ON ---------------- AM	☐ ---------------- AM
OFF ---------------- AM	☐ ---------------- PM
Other:	Other:

General Observation Notes:

Weekly Aquarium Maintenance Log

Name: ______________________________ Start Date: ____________________

Aquarium Purchasa Date: _______________ Number of Fish: _______________

Type of Fish: ____

Item	Details	MON	TUE	WED	THU	FRI	SAT	SUN
Water Change								
Vacuum Gravel								
Clean Filter								
Change Filter								
Clean Impeller								
Change Impeller								
Clean Heater								
Change Heater								
Air Stone Change								
Clean Decorations								
Temperature Check								
Feed Fish								
Fish Medication								

Days

Notes:

____

____

____

____

____

____

____

Weekly Maintenance Log

Maintenance Parameters

Date:

Temperature:	% Water Change:
pH Levels:	Ammonia Levels:
Nitrite Levels:	Nitrate Levels:
Alkalinity Levels:	Salinity Levels:
Phosphate Levels:	Added Water Conditions: Y or N
Light Schedule Time	**Feeding Schedule Times**
ON ---------------- AM	---------------- AM
OFF ---------------- AM	---------------- PM
Other:	Other:

General Observation Notes:

Weekly Aquarium Maintenance Log

Name: ______________________ Start Date: ______________

Aquarium Purchasa Date: __________ Number of Fish: __________

Type of Fish: ____

Item	Details	MON	TUE	WED	THU	FRI	SAT	SUN
Water Change								
Vacuum Gravel								
Clean Filter								
Change Filter								
Clean Impeller								
Change Impeller								
Clean Heater								
Change Heater								
Air Stone Change								
Clean Decorations								
Temperature Check								
Feed Fish								
Fish Medication								

Notes:

Weekly Maintenance Log

Maintenance Parameters

Date:

Temperature:	% Water Change:
pH Levels:	Ammonia Levels:
Nitrite Levels:	Nitrate Levels:
Alkalinity Levels:	Salinity Levels:
Phosphate Levels:	Added Water Conditions: Y or N
Light Schedule Time	**Feeding Schedule Times**
ON ---------------- AM	☐ ---------------- AM
OFF ----------------- AM	☐ ---------------- PM
Other:	Other:

General Observation Notes:

Weekly Aquarium Maintenance Log

Name: ______________________ Start Date: ______________

Aquarium Purchasa Date: __________ Number of Fish: __________

Type of Fish: ____

Item	Details	MON	TUE	WED	THU	FRI	SAT	SUN
Water Change								
Vacuum Gravel								
Clean Filter								
Change Filter								
Clean Impeller								
Change Impeller								
Clean Heater								
Change Heater								
Air Stone Change								
Clean Decorations								
Temperature Check								
Feed Fish								
Fish Medication								

Notes:

Weekly Maintenance Log

Maintenance Parameters

Date:

Temperature:	% Water Change:
pH Levels:	Ammonia Levels:
Nitrite Levels:	Nitrate Levels:
Alkalinity Levels:	Salinity Levels:
Phosphate Levels:	Added Water Conditions: Y or N
Light Schedule Time	**Feeding Schedule Times**
ON --------------- AM	☐ --------------- AM
OFF --------------- AM	☐ --------------- PM
Other:	Other:

General Observation Notes:

Weekly Aquarium Maintenance Log

Name: ______________________ Start Date: ______________

Aquarium Purchasa Date: __________ Number of Fish: __________

Type of Fish: ______________________________________

Item	Details	MON	TUE	WED	THU	FRI	SAT	SUN
Water Change								
Vacuum Gravel								
Clean Filter								
Change Filter								
Clean Impeller								
Change Impeller								
Clean Heater								
Change Heater								
Air Stone Change								
Clean Decorations								
Temperature Check								
Feed Fish								
Fish Medication								

Days

Notes:

Weekly Maintenance Log

Maintenance Parameters

Date:

Temperature:	% Water Change:
pH Levels:	Ammonia Levels:
Nitrite Levels:	Nitrate Levels:
Alkalinity Levels:	Salinity Levels:
Phosphate Levels:	Added Water Conditions: Y or N
Light Schedule Time	**Feeding Schedule Times**
ON ---------------- AM	☐ ---------------- AM
OFF ---------------- AM	☐ ---------------- PM
Other:	Other:

General Observation Notes:

Weekly Aquarium Maintenance Log

Name: ______________________ Start Date: ______________

Aquarium Purchasa Date: __________ Number of Fish: __________

Type of Fish: ____

Item	Details	MON	TUE	WED	THU	FRI	SAT	SUN
Water Change								
Vacuum Gravel								
Clean Filter								
Change Filter								
Clean Impeller								
Change Impeller								
Clean Heater								
Change Heater								
Air Stone Change								
Clean Decorations								
Temperature Check								
Feed Fish								
Fish Medication								

Notes:

Weekly Maintenance Log

Maintenance Parameters

Date:

Temperature:	% Water Change:
pH Levels:	Ammonia Levels:
Nitrite Levels:	Nitrate Levels:
Alkalinity Levels:	Salinity Levels:
Phosphate Levels:	Added Water Conditions: Y or N
Light Schedule Time	**Feeding Schedule Times**
ON ---------------- AM	☐ ---------------- AM
OFF ----------------- AM	☐ ---------------- PM
Other:	Other:

General Observation Notes:

Weekly Aquarium Maintenance Log

Name: ______________________________ Start Date: __________________

Aquarium Purchasa Date: ______________ Number of Fish: ______________

Type of Fish: ____

Item	Details	MON	TUE	WED	THU	FRI	SAT	SUN
Water Change								
Vacuum Gravel								
Clean Filter								
Change Filter								
Clean Impeller								
Change Impeller								
Clean Heater								
Change Heater								
Air Stone Change								
Clean Decorations								
Temperature Check								
Feed Fish								
Fish Medication								

Notes:

Weekly Maintenance Log

Maintenance Parameters

Date:

Temperature:	% Water Change:
pH Levels:	Ammonia Levels:
Nitrite Levels:	Nitrate Levels:
Alkalinity Levels:	Salinity Levels:
Phosphate Levels:	Added Water Conditions: Y or N
Light Schedule Time	**Feeding Schedule Times**
ON --------------- AM	☐ --------------- AM
OFF --------------- AM	☐ --------------- PM
Other:	Other:

General Observation Notes:

Weekly Aquarium Maintenance Log

Name: ______________________ Start Date: ______________

Aquarium Purchasa Date: ____________ Number of Fish: ____________

Type of Fish: ______________________________________

Item	Details	MON	TUE	WED	THU	FRI	SAT	SUN
Water Change								
Vacuum Gravel								
Clean Filter								
Change Filter								
Clean Impeller								
Change Impeller								
Clean Heater								
Change Heater								
Air Stone Change								
Clean Decorations								
Temperature Check								
Feed Fish								
Fish Medication								

Notes:

____

____

____

____

____

____

____

Weekly Maintenance Log

Maintenance Parameters

Date:

Temperature:	% Water Change:
pH Levels:	Ammonia Levels:
Nitrite Levels:	Nitrate Levels:
Alkalinity Levels:	Salinity Levels:
Phosphate Levels:	Added Water Conditions: Y or N
Light Schedule Time	**Feeding Schedule Times**
ON ---------------- AM	☐ ---------------- AM
OFF ---------------- AM	☐ ---------------- PM
Other:	Other:

General Observation Notes:

____

____

____

____

____

____

____

____

____

____

____

____

____

____

Weekly Aquarium Maintenance Log

Name: ______________________ Start Date: ______________

Aquarium Purchasa Date: ____________ Number of Fish: ____________

Type of Fish: ______________________________________

Item	Details	MON	TUE	WED	THU	FRI	SAT	SUN
Water Change								
Vacuum Gravel								
Clean Filter								
Change Filter								
Clean Impeller								
Change Impeller								
Clean Heater								
Change Heater								
Air Stone Change								
Clean Decorations								
Temperature Check								
Feed Fish								
Fish Medication								

Notes:

____

____

____

____

____

____

____

Weekly Maintenance Log

Maintenance Parameters

Date:

Temperature:	% Water Change:
pH Levels:	Ammonia Levels:
Nitrite Levels:	Nitrate Levels:
Alkalinity Levels:	Salinity Levels:
Phosphate Levels:	Added Water Conditions: Y or N
Light Schedule Time	**Feeding Schedule Times**
ON ---------------- AM	☐ ---------------- AM
OFF ---------------- AM	☐ ---------------- PM
Other:	Other:

General Observation Notes:

Weekly Aquarium Maintenance Log

Name: ______________________ Start Date: ______________

Aquarium Purchasa Date: __________ Number of Fish: __________

Type of Fish: ______________________________

Item	Details	MON	TUE	WED	THU	FRI	SAT	SUN
Water Change								
Vacuum Gravel								
Clean Filter								
Change Filter								
Clean Impeller								
Change Impeller								
Clean Heater								
Change Heater								
Air Stone Change								
Clean Decorations								
Temperature Check								
Feed Fish								
Fish Medication								

Notes:

Weekly Maintenance Log

Maintenance Parameters

Date:

Temperature:	% Water Change:
pH Levels:	Ammonia Levels:
Nitrite Levels:	Nitrate Levels:
Alkalinity Levels:	Salinity Levels:
Phosphate Levels:	Added Water Conditions: Y or N
Light Schedule Time	**Feeding Schedule Times**
ON ---------------- AM	---------------- AM
OFF ---------------- AM	---------------- PM
Other:	Other:

General Observation Notes:

Weekly Aquarium Maintenance Log

Name: ______________________________ Start Date: ____________________

Aquarium Purchasa Date: ______________ Number of Fish: ______________

Type of Fish: ____

Item	Details	MON	TUE	WED	THU	FRI	SAT	SUN
Water Change								
Vacuum Gravel								
Clean Filter								
Change Filter								
Clean Impeller								
Change Impeller								
Clean Heater								
Change Heater								
Air Stone Change								
Clean Decorations								
Temperature Check								
Feed Fish								
Fish Medication								

(Days)

Notes:

____

____

____

____

____

____

____

Weekly Maintenance Log

Maintenance Parameters

Date:

Temperature:	% Water Change:
pH Levels:	Ammonia Levels:
Nitrite Levels:	Nitrate Levels:
Alkalinity Levels:	Salinity Levels:
Phosphate Levels:	Added Water Conditions: Y or N
Light Schedule Time	**Feeding Schedule Times**
ON ---------------- AM	☐ ---------------- AM
OFF ---------------- AM	☐ ---------------- PM
Other:	Other:

General Observation Notes:

Weekly Aquarium Maintenance Log

Name: ______________________ Start Date: ______________

Aquarium Purchasa Date: ____________ Number of Fish: ____________

Type of Fish: ____

Item	Details	MON	TUE	WED	THU	FRI	SAT	SUN
Water Change								
Vacuum Gravel								
Clean Filter								
Change Filter								
Clean Impeller								
Change Impeller								
Clean Heater								
Change Heater								
Air Stone Change								
Clean Decorations								
Temperature Check								
Feed Fish								
Fish Medication								

Notes:

____

____

____

____

____

____

____

Weekly Maintenance Log

Maintenance Parameters

Date:

Temperature:	% Water Change:
pH Levels:	Ammonia Levels:
Nitrite Levels:	Nitrate Levels:
Alkalinity Levels:	Salinity Levels:
Phosphate Levels:	Added Water Conditions: Y or N
Light Schedule Time	**Feeding Schedule Times**
ON ---------------- AM	☐ ---------------- AM
OFF ----------------- AM	☐ ---------------- PM
Other:	Other:

General Observation Notes:

Weekly Aquarium Maintenance Log

Name: ______________________ Start Date: ______________

Aquarium Purchasa Date: __________ Number of Fish: __________

Type of Fish: ______________________________________

Item	Details	MON	TUE	WED	THU	FRI	SAT	SUN
Water Change								
Vacuum Gravel								
Clean Filter								
Change Filter								
Clean Impeller								
Change Impeller								
Clean Heater								
Change Heater								
Air Stone Change								
Clean Decorations								
Temperature Check								
Feed Fish								
Fish Medication								

Notes:

Weekly Maintenance Log

Maintenance Parameters

Date:

Temperature:	% Water Change:
pH Levels:	Ammonia Levels:
Nitrite Levels:	Nitrate Levels:
Alkalinity Levels:	Salinity Levels:
Phosphate Levels:	Added Water Conditions: Y or N
Light Schedule Time	**Feeding Schedule Times**
ON ---------------- AM	☐ ---------------- AM
OFF ---------------- AM	☐ ---------------- PM
Other:	Other:

General Observation Notes:

Weekly Aquarium Maintenance Log

Name: ______________________ Start Date: ______________

Aquarium Purchasa Date: ____________ Number of Fish: ____________

Type of Fish: ____

Item	Details	Days						
		MON	TUE	WED	THU	FRI	SAT	SUN
Water Change								
Vacuum Gravel								
Clean Filter								
Change Filter								
Clean Impeller								
Change Impeller								
Clean Heater								
Change Heater								
Air Stone Change								
Clean Decorations								
Temperature Check								
Feed Fish								
Fish Medication								

Notes:

____

____

____

____

____

____

____

Weekly Maintenance Log

Maintenance Parameters

Date:

Temperature:	% Water Change:
pH Levels:	Ammonia Levels:
Nitrite Levels:	Nitrate Levels:
Alkalinity Levels:	Salinity Levels:
Phosphate Levels:	Added Water Conditions: Y or N
Light Schedule Time	**Feeding Schedule Times**
ON ---------------- AM	☐ ---------------- AM
OFF ---------------- AM	☐ ---------------- PM
Other:	Other:

General Observation Notes:

Weekly Aquarium Maintenance Log

Name: ______________________________ Start Date: ____________________

Aquarium Purchasa Date: ______________ Number of Fish: ______________

Type of Fish: ____

Item	Details	MON	TUE	WED	THU	FRI	SAT	SUN
Water Change								
Vacuum Gravel								
Clean Filter								
Change Filter								
Clean Impeller								
Change Impeller								
Clean Heater								
Change Heater								
Air Stone Change								
Clean Decorations								
Temperature Check								
Feed Fish								
Fish Medication								

Notes:

____

____

____

____

____

____

____

Weekly Maintenance Log

Maintenance Parameters

Date:

Temperature:	% Water Change:
pH Levels:	Ammonia Levels:
Nitrite Levels:	Nitrate Levels:
Alkalinity Levels:	Salinity Levels:
Phosphate Levels:	Added Water Conditions: Y or N
Light Schedule Time	**Feeding Schedule Times**
ON --------------- AM	☐ --------------- AM
OFF ---------------- AM	☐ --------------- PM
Other:	Other:

General Observation Notes:

____

____

____

____

____

____

____

____

____

____

____

____

____

____

Weekly Aquarium Maintenance Log

Name: ______________________ Start Date: ______________

Aquarium Purchasa Date: ____________ Number of Fish: ____________

Type of Fish: ______________________________________

Item	Details	MON	TUE	WED	THU	FRI	SAT	SUN
Water Change								
Vacuum Gravel								
Clean Filter								
Change Filter								
Clean Impeller								
Change Impeller								
Clean Heater								
Change Heater								
Air Stone Change								
Clean Decorations								
Temperature Check								
Feed Fish								
Fish Medication								

Notes:

Weekly Maintenance Log

Maintenance Parameters

Date:

Temperature:	% Water Change:
pH Levels:	Ammonia Levels:
Nitrite Levels:	Nitrate Levels:
Alkalinity Levels:	Salinity Levels:
Phosphate Levels:	Added Water Conditions: Y or N
Light Schedule Time	**Feeding Schedule Times**
ON ---------------- AM	☐ ---------------- AM
OFF ----------------- AM	☐ ---------------- PM
Other:	Other:

General Observation Notes:

Weekly Aquarium Maintenance Log

Name: ______________________ Start Date: ______________

Aquarium Purchasa Date: ___________ Number of Fish: ___________

Type of Fish: ____

Item	Details	MON	TUE	WED	THU	FRI	SAT	SUN
Water Change								
Vacuum Gravel								
Clean Filter								
Change Filter								
Clean Impeller								
Change Impeller								
Clean Heater								
Change Heater								
Air Stone Change								
Clean Decorations								
Temperature Check								
Feed Fish								
Fish Medication								

Notes:

Weekly Maintenance Log

Maintenance Parameters

Date:

Temperature:	% Water Change:
pH Levels:	Ammonia Levels:
Nitrite Levels:	Nitrate Levels:
Alkalinity Levels:	Salinity Levels:
Phosphate Levels:	Added Water Conditions: Y or N
Light Schedule Time	**Feeding Schedule Times**
ON ---------------- AM	☐ ---------------- AM
OFF ----------------- AM	☐ ---------------- PM
Other:	Other:

General Observation Notes:

Weekly Aquarium Maintenance Log

Name: ______________________ Start Date: ______________

Aquarium Purchasa Date: ____________ Number of Fish: __________

Type of Fish: ______________________________________

Item	Details	MON	TUE	WED	THU	FRI	SAT	SUN
Water Change								
Vacuum Gravel								
Clean Filter								
Change Filter								
Clean Impeller								
Change Impeller								
Clean Heater								
Change Heater								
Air Stone Change								
Clean Decorations								
Temperature Check								
Feed Fish								
Fish Medication								

Notes:

____

____

____

____

____

____

____

Weekly Maintenance Log

Maintenance Parameters

Date:

Temperature:	% Water Change:
pH Levels:	Ammonia Levels:
Nitrite Levels:	Nitrate Levels:
Alkalinity Levels:	Salinity Levels:
Phosphate Levels:	Added Water Conditions: Y or N
Light Schedule Time	**Feeding Schedule Times**
ON ---------------- AM	☐ ---------------- AM
OFF ----------------- AM	☐ ---------------- PM
Other:	Other:

General Observation Notes:

____

____

____

____

____

____

____

____

____

____

____

____

____

____

Weekly Aquarium Maintenance Log

Name: ______________________ Start Date: ______________________

Aquarium Purchasa Date: ______________________ Number of Fish: ______________________

Type of Fish: ____

Item	Details	Days						
		MON	TUE	WED	THU	FRI	SAT	SUN
Water Change								
Vacuum Gravel								
Clean Filter								
Change Filter								
Clean Impeller								
Change Impeller								
Clean Heater								
Change Heater								
Air Stone Change								
Clean Decorations								
Temperature Check								
Feed Fish								
Fish Medication								

Notes:

Weekly Maintenance Log

Maintenance Parameters

Date:

Temperature:	% Water Change:
pH Levels:	Ammonia Levels:
Nitrite Levels:	Nitrate Levels:
Alkalinity Levels:	Salinity Levels:
Phosphate Levels:	Added Water Conditions: Y or N
Light Schedule Time	**Feeding Schedule Times**
ON ---------------- AM	☐ ---------------- AM
OFF ---------------- AM	☐ ---------------- PM
Other:	Other:

General Observation Notes:

Weekly Aquarium Maintenance Log

Name: ______________________ Start Date: ______________

Aquarium Purchasa Date: ____________ Number of Fish: ____________

Type of Fish: ____

Item	Details	MON	TUE	WED	THU	FRI	SAT	SUN
Water Change								
Vacuum Gravel								
Clean Filter								
Change Filter								
Clean Impeller								
Change Impeller								
Clean Heater								
Change Heater								
Air Stone Change								
Clean Decorations								
Temperature Check								
Feed Fish								
Fish Medication								

Notes:

Weekly Maintenance Log

Maintenance Parameters

Date:

Temperature:	% Water Change:
pH Levels:	Ammonia Levels:
Nitrite Levels:	Nitrate Levels:
Alkalinity Levels:	Salinity Levels:
Phosphate Levels:	Added Water Conditions: Y or N
Light Schedule Time	**Feeding Schedule Times**
ON ---------------- AM	☐ ---------------- AM
OFF ---------------- AM	☐ ---------------- PM
Other:	Other:

General Observation Notes:

_____
_____
_____
_____
_____
_____
_____
_____
_____
_____
_____
_____

Weekly Aquarium Maintenance Log

Name: ______________________ Start Date: ______________

Aquarium Purchasa Date: ___________ Number of Fish: ___________

Type of Fish: ______________________________

Item	Details	MON	TUE	WED	THU	FRI	SAT	SUN
Water Change								
Vacuum Gravel								
Clean Filter								
Change Filter								
Clean Impeller								
Change Impeller								
Clean Heater								
Change Heater								
Air Stone Change								
Clean Decorations								
Temperature Check								
Feed Fish								
Fish Medication								

Notes:

Weekly Maintenance Log

Maintenance Parameters

Date:

Temperature:	% Water Change:
pH Levels:	Ammonia Levels:
Nitrite Levels:	Nitrate Levels:
Alkalinity Levels:	Salinity Levels:
Phosphate Levels:	Added Water Conditions: Y or N
Light Schedule Time	**Feeding Schedule Times**
ON --------------- AM	☐ --------------- AM
OFF --------------- AM	☐ --------------- PM
Other:	Other:

General Observation Notes:

Weekly Aquarium Maintenance Log

Name: ______________________________ Start Date: ___________________

Aquarium Purchasa Date: ______________ Number of Fish: ______________

Type of Fish: ____

Item	Details	MON	TUE	WED	THU	FRI	SAT	SUN
Water Change								
Vacuum Gravel								
Clean Filter								
Change Filter								
Clean Impeller								
Change Impeller								
Clean Heater								
Change Heater								
Air Stone Change								
Clean Decorations								
Temperature Check								
Feed Fish								
Fish Medication								

Notes:

Weekly Maintenance Log

Maintenance Parameters

Date:

Temperature:	% Water Change:
pH Levels:	Ammonia Levels:
Nitrite Levels:	Nitrate Levels:
Alkalinity Levels:	Salinity Levels:
Phosphate Levels:	Added Water Conditions: Y or N
Light Schedule Time	**Feeding Schedule Times**
ON ---------------- AM	---------------- AM
OFF ----------------- AM	---------------- PM
Other:	Other:

General Observation Notes:

Weekly Aquarium Maintenance Log

Name: ______________________ Start Date: ______________

Aquarium Purchasa Date: __________ Number of Fish: __________

Type of Fish: ____

Item	Details	MON	TUE	WED	THU	FRI	SAT	SUN
Water Change								
Vacuum Gravel								
Clean Filter								
Change Filter								
Clean Impeller								
Change Impeller								
Clean Heater								
Change Heater								
Air Stone Change								
Clean Decorations								
Temperature Check								
Feed Fish								
Fish Medication								

Notes:

Weekly Maintenance Log

Maintenance Parameters

Date:

Temperature:	% Water Change:
pH Levels:	Ammonia Levels:
Nitrite Levels:	Nitrate Levels:
Alkalinity Levels:	Salinity Levels:
Phosphate Levels:	Added Water Conditions: Y or N
Light Schedule Time	**Feeding Schedule Times**
ON ---------------- AM	☐ ---------------- AM
OFF ---------------- AM	☐ ---------------- PM
Other:	Other:

General Observation Notes:

Weekly Aquarium Maintenance Log

Name: ______________________ Start Date: ______________

Aquarium Purchasa Date: __________ Number of Fish: __________

Type of Fish: ______________________________________

Item	Details	MON	TUE	WED	THU	FRI	SAT	SUN
Water Change								
Vacuum Gravel								
Clean Filter								
Change Filter								
Clean Impeller								
Change Impeller								
Clean Heater								
Change Heater								
Air Stone Change								
Clean Decorations								
Temperature Check								
Feed Fish								
Fish Medication								

Notes:

Weekly Maintenance Log

Maintenance Parameters

Date:

Temperature:	% Water Change:
pH Levels:	Ammonia Levels:
Nitrite Levels:	Nitrate Levels:
Alkalinity Levels:	Salinity Levels:
Phosphate Levels:	Added Water Conditions: Y or N
Light Schedule Time	**Feeding Schedule Times**
ON ---------------- AM	☐ ---------------- AM
OFF ---------------- AM	☐ ---------------- PM
Other:	Other:

General Observation Notes:

Weekly Aquarium Maintenance Log

Name: ______________________________ Start Date: __________________

Aquarium Purchasa Date: ______________ Number of Fish: ______________

Type of Fish: ____

Item	Details	Days MON	TUE	WED	THU	FRI	SAT	SUN
Water Change								
Vacuum Gravel								
Clean Filter								
Change Filter								
Clean Impeller								
Change Impeller								
Clean Heater								
Change Heater								
Air Stone Change								
Clean Decorations								
Temperature Check								
Feed Fish								
Fish Medication								

Notes:

Weekly Maintenance Log

Maintenance Parameters

Date:

Temperature:	% Water Change:
pH Levels:	Ammonia Levels:
Nitrite Levels:	Nitrate Levels:
Alkalinity Levels:	Salinity Levels:
Phosphate Levels:	Added Water Conditions: Y or N
Light Schedule Time	**Feeding Schedule Times**
ON ---------------- AM	☐ ---------------- AM
OFF ---------------- AM	☐ ---------------- PM
Other:	Other:

General Observation Notes:

Weekly Aquarium Maintenance Log

Name: ______________________ Start Date: ______________

Aquarium Purchasa Date: ____________ Number of Fish: ____________

Type of Fish: ______________________________________

Item	Details	MON	TUE	WED	THU	FRI	SAT	SUN
Water Change								
Vacuum Gravel								
Clean Filter								
Change Filter								
Clean Impeller								
Change Impeller								
Clean Heater								
Change Heater								
Air Stone Change								
Clean Decorations								
Temperature Check								
Feed Fish								
Fish Medication								

Notes:

Weekly Maintenance Log

Maintenance Parameters

Date:

Temperature:	% Water Change:
pH Levels:	Ammonia Levels:
Nitrite Levels:	Nitrate Levels:
Alkalinity Levels:	Salinity Levels:
Phosphate Levels:	Added Water Conditions: Y or N
Light Schedule Time	**Feeding Schedule Times**
ON ---------------- AM	☐ ---------------- AM
OFF ----------------- AM	☐ ---------------- PM
Other:	Other:

General Observation Notes:

Weekly Aquarium Maintenance Log

Name: ____________________ Start Date: ____________________

Aquarium Purchasa Date: ____________________ Number of Fish: ____________________

Type of Fish: ____________________

Item	Details	MON	TUE	WED	THU	FRI	SAT	SUN
Water Change								
Vacuum Gravel								
Clean Filter								
Change Filter								
Clean Impeller								
Change Impeller								
Clean Heater								
Change Heater								
Air Stone Change								
Clean Decorations								
Temperature Check								
Feed Fish								
Fish Medication								

Notes:

Weekly Maintenance Log

Maintenance Parameters

Date:

Temperature:	% Water Change:
pH Levels:	Ammonia Levels:
Nitrite Levels:	Nitrate Levels:
Alkalinity Levels:	Salinity Levels:
Phosphate Levels:	Added Water Conditions: Y or N
Light Schedule Time	**Feeding Schedule Times**
ON ---------------- AM	☐ ---------------- AM
OFF ---------------- AM	☐ ---------------- PM
Other:	Other:

General Observation Notes:

Weekly Aquarium Maintenance Log

Name: _____   Start Date: _____
Aquarium Purchasa Date: _____   Number of Fish: _____
Type of Fish: _____

Days

Item	Details	MON	TUE	WED	THU	FRI	SAT	SUN
Water Change		☐	☐	☐	☐	☐	☐	☐
Vacuum Gravel		☐	☐	☐	☐	☐	☐	☐
Clean Filter		☐	☐	☐	☐	☐	☐	☐
Change Filter		☐	☐	☐	☐	☐	☐	☐
Clean Impeller		☐	☐	☐	☐	☐	☐	☐
Change Impeller		☐	☐	☐	☐	☐	☐	☐
Clean Heater		☐	☐	☐	☐	☐	☐	☐
Change Heater		☐	☐	☐	☐	☐	☐	☐
Air Stone Change		☐	☐	☐	☐	☐	☐	☐
Clean Decorations		☐	☐	☐	☐	☐	☐	☐
Temperature Check		☐	☐	☐	☐	☐	☐	☐
Feed Fish		☐	☐	☐	☐	☐	☐	☐
Fish Medication		☐	☐	☐	☐	☐	☐	☐

Notes:

_____
_____
_____
_____
_____
_____

Weekly Maintenance Log

Maintenance Parameters

Date:

Temperature:	% Water Change:
pH Levels:	Ammonia Levels:
Nitrite Levels:	Nitrate Levels:
Alkalinity Levels:	Salinity Levels:
Phosphate Levels:	Added Water Conditions: Y or N
Light Schedule Time	**Feeding Schedule Times**
ON --------------- AM	☐ --------------- AM
OFF --------------- AM	☐ --------------- PM
Other:	Other:

General Observation Notes:

____

____

____

____

____

____

____

____

____

____

____

____

____

____

Weekly Aquarium Maintenance Log

Name: ______________________ Start Date: ______________

Aquarium Purchasa Date: ______________ Number of Fish: ______________

Type of Fish: ______________________________________

Item	Details	MON	TUE	WED	THU	FRI	SAT	SUN
Water Change								
Vacuum Gravel								
Clean Filter								
Change Filter								
Clean Impeller								
Change Impeller								
Clean Heater								
Change Heater								
Air Stone Change								
Clean Decorations								
Temperature Check								
Feed Fish								
Fish Medication								

Notes:

Weekly Maintenance Log

Maintenance Parameters

Date:

Temperature:	% Water Change:
pH Levels:	Ammonia Levels:
Nitrite Levels:	Nitrate Levels:
Alkalinity Levels:	Salinity Levels:
Phosphate Levels:	Added Water Conditions: Y or N
Light Schedule Time	**Feeding Schedule Times**
ON --------------- AM	☐ --------------- AM
OFF --------------- AM	☐ --------------- PM
Other:	Other:

General Observation Notes:

Weekly Aquarium Maintenance Log

Name: ______________________________ Start Date: ____________________

Aquarium Purchasa Date: ______________ Number of Fish: ______________

Type of Fish: ____

Item	Details	MON	TUE	WED	THU	FRI	SAT	SUN
Water Change								
Vacuum Gravel								
Clean Filter								
Change Filter								
Clean Impeller								
Change Impeller								
Clean Heater								
Change Heater								
Air Stone Change								
Clean Decorations								
Temperature Check								
Feed Fish								
Fish Medication								

Notes:

____

____

____

____

____

____

____

We want to thank you for purchasing this book. Our writers and creative team took pride in creating this book, and we have tried to make it as enjoyable as possible.

We would love to hear from you, kindly leave a review if you enjoyed this book so we can do more. Your reviews on our books are highly appreciated. Also, if you have any comments or suggestions, you may reach us at

info@contentarcade.com

Regards,
Content Arcade Publishing Team

Made in the USA
Monee, IL
13 December 2020

52806015R00056